HORSES SET II

MUSTANG HORSES

Kristin Van Cleaf
ABDO Publishing Company

visit us at
www.abdopub.com

Published by ABDO Publishing Company, 4940 Viking Drive, Edina, Minnesota 55435.
Copyright © 2006 by Abdo Consulting Group, Inc. International copyrights reserved in all
countries. No part of this book may be reproduced in any form without written permission from
the publisher. The Checkerboard Library™ is a trademark and logo of ABDO Publishing
Company.

Printed in the United States.

Cover Photo: Corbis
Interior Photos: Corbis pp. 7, 9; John Eastcott and Yva Momatiuk / National Geographic pp. 10,
    11, 13, 14, 15, 19; Landon Nordeman / National Geographic p. 21; Yva Momatiuk and John
    Eastcott / Minden Pictures pp. 5, 17

Series Coordinator: Heidi M. Dahmes
Editors: Heidi M. Dahmes, Megan M. Gunderson
Art Direction: Neil Klinepier

Library of Congress Cataloging-in-Publication Data

Van Cleaf, Kristin, 1976-
    Mustang horses / Kristin Van Cleaf.
        p. cm. -- (Horses. Set II)
    Includes bibliographical references.
    ISBN 1-59679-316-3
        1. Mustang--Juvenile literature. I. Title.

SF293.M9V36 2005
599.665'5--dc22

                                                    2005045797

CONTENTS

WHERE MUSTANGS CAME FROM

Horses are strong animals with good hearing and eyesight. They developed from a fox-sized animal called eohippus.

Over time, humans learned the value of horses. The animals could plow farmland, pull carts, and perform other tasks. So, people brought horses all over the world.

Spaniards first brought horses to the New World in the 1500s. They found no horses there. Horses had disappeared from this region. The Spaniards left behind many of their horses. And, many escaped into the wild.

Horses changed the lives of Native Americans. These people had never seen the animals before and found them useful. Horses became an important part of Native American culture.

Today, **descendants** of the Spanish horses are known as mustangs. This word comes from the Spanish word for a stray horse. Now, it is the name used for wild horses in the United States.

Mustangs were used as cow horses and as army horses.

WHAT MUSTANGS LOOK LIKE

Horses are measured in four-inch (10-cm) units called hands. This measurement is taken from the highest point of the back, called the withers, to the ground.

Mustangs have a medium-sized body. An average mustang stands about 14.2 hands high. At this height, it weighs about 600 to 800 pounds (270 to 360 kg). However, some are as short as 13 hands or as tall as 16 hands.

These wild horses have short backs, rounded rumps, and low-set tails. They have strong, hard feet. They possess a Spanish-type head. The mustang's Spanish-type head is broad with a narrow face. And, its ears are short and curve toward each other.

Mustangs still display certain features from their Spanish ancestors.

What Makes Mustangs Special

Settlers brought horses with them as they moved into the western United States. Some horses escaped or were turned loose by failed ranchers.

In the early 1900s, more than 2 million mustangs wandered the western United States. Ranchers valued these horses for their speed and endurance. Then, farming practices began to change. By the 1920s, tractors had replaced horses.

Wild horses were soon seen as pests. So, the U.S. government authorized removal of the horses. And, people began killing them. Soon, fewer than 17,000 mustangs remained.

In 1971, the U.S. Congress passed the Wild Free-Roaming Horse and Burro Act. This act protects, manages, and controls these animals. Today, about 39,000 wild horses roam the West.

The Bureau of Land Management monitors the sizes of mustang herds. Each year, thousands of wild horses are captured and put up for adoption.

Horses roam on land controlled by the Bureau of Land Management.

COLOR

Mustangs come in a variety of colors and sizes. Most often, mustangs are sorrel or bay in color. They can also be roan, black, white, paint, brown and grullo, and dun

and gray. Mustangs tend to have a black mane and tail.

Grooming helps keep a tamed mustang's coat healthy and looking nice. Brushing removes dirt and **dandruff**. If kept in a stable, your mustang should be groomed every day. This can be done with a body brush, a currycomb, and a mane and tail comb.

If you adopt a mustang while it is young, that is a good time to get it used to regular grooming and handling.

10

Mustangs exhibit a variety of coat patterns as well as colors.

CARE

Many mustangs are born wild. They roam the prairies, finding their own shelter and food. But if a person adopts a mustang, he or she must provide shelter and care for the horse.

A stable or barn will provide a tamed mustang with shelter. The horse should be able to move around comfortably while inside its stall. The area should be kept clean and dry. And, it should have fresh air.

A mustang can sleep standing up. But, the stall's floor should be made more comfortable with bedding. This can be wood shavings, straw, or sawdust.

Look at the horse's hooves daily. Remove stones, dirt, or other objects from the bottom of the feet with a hoof pick. Mustangs have strong feet, so they may not need horseshoes. Normally, horseshoes are used to protect a horse's feet from hard surfaces.

Like young people, these horses enjoy play fighting.

Properly caring for a mustang will prevent many health problems. Regular exercise is a must. Watch for signs of illness. A mustang will need a checkup with a veterinarian at least once a year. It should receive **vaccines**. And, your horse's teeth may need to be **floated**.

FEEDING

Part of caring for a tamed mustang is providing it with food and water. Horses eat hay, grass, and grain. Keep the hay in a net or rack. Be sure to keep it dry to prevent mold.

Grass is a horse's natural food.

Grain provides a working mustang with more energy than hay alone. Grain can be oats, corn, and barley. This feed is usually provided in a feed bin or a feed **trough**.

Tamed mustangs may also need vitamins and other **supplements**. Salt is one of the most important. Horses lose salt when they sweat. So, mustangs will need a block of salt to lick.

A clean, running stream is a perfect water source for these wild horses.

A mustang also needs fresh, clean water. It can drink from a watering trough or even a fountain in the stall. It will drink about ten gallons (38 L) of water in a day.

THINGS MUSTANGS NEED

A tamed mustang's equipment is called tack. It is important to use tack that fits well and is clean. Clean tack will not irritate the horse or cause other problems.

A bridle is used to control a mustang. It is made up of leather straps that fit over the horse's head. The straps are attached to reins and a bit. The bit is a piece of metal that sits in the horse's mouth.

Saddles come in two types for U.S. riders. A western saddle is best for working horses. It has a **horn** and wide **stirrups**. An English saddle is lighter and flatter. It makes racing and fence jumping easier.

A saddle is laid on top of a saddle pad. The pad may be rectangular or saddle shaped. It protects the mustang's back and sides from the rubbing of the saddle. It also keeps dirt and sweat from irritating the horse's skin.

Adopted mustangs need a lot of love and patience.

How Mustangs Grow

A female horse is called a mare. If she becomes **pregnant**, she will carry the baby inside her for about 11 months. Typically, horses have one baby at a time.

A baby horse is called a foal. A mustang foal is born with long legs. It should stand within an hour of its birth. A mustang foal will follow its mother around. In just a day, the foal will be running. But it uses up its energy quickly, so it needs a lot of rest.

For about two months, a mustang foal drinks its mother's milk and eats grass. Toward the end of that time, the foal should be sharing the mare's feed. When the foal is about four and a half to six months old, it will be **weaned** from its mother.

A mare will help her foal to drink her milk. The foal must have its first drink within 24 hours.

TRAINING

Training a mustang requires patience. Because they were once wild, these horses are suspicious of people. It can take a while for mustangs to become used to humans.

A trainer needs to gain a mustang's trust before the horse can be trained. Trainers use slow, calm movements to gentle the horse. The trainers are tender, but firm. Once trust is gained and the horse is gentled, a mustang can be trained.

Horses learn by conditioning. For example, a trainer sitting on a horse will squeeze his or her legs. The trainer will stop squeezing his or her legs when the horse gives the desired response. Repeating these actions teaches the mustang what the right response is.

The horse will learn to walk, trot, and gallop on command. A gentled, or trained, mustang may work on a ranch or in a **rodeo**. And, it makes a good family horse.

Mustangs are easily spooked. So, they need patient trainers.

GLOSSARY

dandruff - scaly flakes of dead skin that come from the scalp.

descendant - a person or animal that comes from a particular ancestor or group of ancestors.

float - to file down a horse's teeth in order to remove sharp edges.

horn - a projection from a saddle that is used for tying a rope around.

pregnant - having one or more babies growing within the body.

rodeo - a show featuring cattle roping, bronco riding, or steer wrestling.

stirrup - one of a pair of loops or rings hanging from a saddle used as footholds to help in mounting and riding.

supplement - something that improves or completes something else.

trough - a long, shallow container for the drinking water or feed of domestic animals.

vaccine (vak-SEEN) - a shot given to animals or humans to prevent them from getting an illness or disease.

wean - to accustom an animal to eat food other than its mother's milk.

WEB SITES

To learn more about mustangs, visit ABDO Publishing Company on the World Wide Web at **www.abdopub.com**. Web sites about these horses are featured on our Book Links page. These links are routinely monitored and updated to provide the most current information available.

INDEX